This book belongs to

....

For my own Corin
and Jordan—C. H.

For Wren, with love
from Tor—T. F.

Brimming with creative inspiration, how-to projects, and useful information to enrich your everyday life, Quarto Knows is a favorite destination for those pursuing their interests and passions. Visit our site and dig deeper with our books into your area of interest: Quarto Creates, Quarto Cooks, Quarto Homes, Quarto Lives, Quarto Drives, Quarto Explores, Quarto Gifts, or Quarto Kids.

Inspiring | Educating | Creating | Entertaining

Text © 2020 Colette Hiller. Illustrations © 2020 Tor Freeman.
First published in 2020 by Frances Lincoln Children's Books, an imprint of The Quarto Group. 100 Cummings Center, Suite 265D, Beverly, MA 01915, USA.
T +1 978-282-9590 F +1 078-283-2742 www.QuartoKnows.com
The right of Colette Hiller to be identified as the author
and Tor Freeman to be identified as the illustrator of this work has been
asserted by them in accordance with the Copyright,
Designs and Act, 1988 (United Kingdom).

A catalogue record for this book is available from the British Library.
ISBN 978-0-7112-5460-2
The illustrations were created with graphite and colored pencil.
Set in Pelham D Infant.
Published by Katie Cotton. Designed by Zoë Tucker.
Production by Caragh McAleenan.
Manufactured in Guangdong, China TT042021

5 7 9 8 6 4

MIX
Paper from
responsible sources
FSC® C016973
FSC
www.fsc.org

Contents

How to use this book 6

Sounds

Silent Letters and Secrets

Spellings

Words that Sound the Same

HOW TO USE THIS BOOK

This is a collection of rhymes to help children learn to read and spell. There are ditties for children just mastering letter sounds, and magic spells for more able readers. Using wordplay, rhythm, and a dash of silliness, these rhymes boost literacy and thinking skills. But most of all, they aim to delight children, to spark imagination, and instil a love of the English language.

BE A CHERRY PICKER!

You don't need to teach these rhymes in any particular order!
Just choose a rhyme that you think your child will enjoy.

GET READY

Before reading a rhyme aloud, spend a few minutes helping your child explore the learning concept behind it. Some lively, simple activities are included at the back of this book.

TIP FOR READING ALOUD

Rhymes include the names of letters as well as the sounds that they make. For a rhyme to scan, here's the plan: when you see capitalized letters separated by a dash, pronounce each letter by its name. For example, if you see O-U-T say the names of all three letters (rather than the word "out").

FIND THE BEAT

The rhythms are based on simple chants. Imagine a clock ticking steadily behind you!

REPEAT AND REPEAT!

Read a rhyme lots of times so that your child can join in.

NOW DISCUSS

The illustrations underpin the message of the rhyme.
There are things to talk about and for your child to find.

JUST A FEW THAT ARE NEW

The learning concept behind a rhyme may take time to absorb.
Read just a few at a time.

HAVE A GOOD OLD TIME OF IT!

Have fun with this and your child will too!

A NOTE TO YOUNG READERS

The grown up reading this book with you
is trying to find the rhythm.
But if they should happen to make a mistake,
please do your best to forgive them.
Politely suggest that they start once again,
with *feeling* so you understand.
By tapping your feet, you can help keep the beat
and join in whenever you can!
If they try hard, and do a good job,
encourage them with a, "Well done!"
Learning to read is an absolute breeze,
now go have some fabulous fun.

'*The B On Your Thumb* is clever, engaging, educational and fun. I wish I had thought of it.'

—Craig Smith, author / song writer of *The Wonky Donkey*

'Wonderful rhymes and hilarious illustrations... Parents, teachers, and children will find this book entertaining and useful.'

—Bonnie Macmillan, author of *Teach A Child to Read in One Week*

'I can't think of a more enjoyable way to learn.'

—Dr Susan B Neuman, education policy maker and Professor of Literacy Education, NYU

'*The B on Your Thumb*
is your number-one chum –
    a magical spell for excelling.
The rhymes are a riot,
so come on and try it –
    you'll soon be a wizard at spelling.'

—Dennis Lee, author of the award-winning classic, *Alligator Pie*

'. . . Colette Hiller's poems are a pedagogical gift. Joyful reading lessons– with a phonological lift.'

—Timothy Shanahan, Distinguished Professor Emeritus at the University of Illinois and government policy advisor on literacy education

Sounds

Some letters sound as they are meant to.

Other letters change.

They sometimes make surprising noises.

English can be strange!

The Sh in Your Shoe

Once there was an S
who usually went ssss . . .
Along came an H.
Together they went shhh . . .

S and H go sh,
that is what they do.
The sh that's in your shoulder,
the sh that's in your shoe.
S and H go sh,
that is what they do.

The sh that's in your shower,
the sh in your shampoo.
S and H go sh,
that is what they do.
S and H go sh,
which isn't very loud,
but S and H can also make a . . .
sh sh sh... SHOUT!

See with Two Es

Use your two eyes
to see with two Es.
Do you see the cheetah
there in the trees?
Do you see his teeth,
sharp as can be?
See with two Es
how fast you can flee!

O-U are Inside Out

O-U can really shout.
O-U are inside out.
O-U are all about.
And you are O-U-T spells out!

O-U are on the ground.
O-U are all around.
O-U can really pout.
And you are O-U-T spells out!

Oi!

Join this famous chant of joy:
oggy, oggy, oggy, oi, oi, oi!
Use your voice and make some noise:
oggy, oggy, oggy, oi, oi, oi!
It's just something grown-ups say:
oggy, oggy, oggy, oi, oi, oi!
There's no point, but anyway:
oggy, oggy, oggy,
oi, oi, oi!

The Story of Q and U

Q met U
while in a queue
waiting for
a bus.

Q looked at U
and then he knew.
He knew he was
in love.

"How I love U,"
announced the Q.
"Let's always
be together."

QUILTS

QUALITY
CROWNS
FOR
QUEENS!

"I love Q too,"
replied the U.
"I'll be your queen forever."

And so the two,
the Q and U,
they quickly
made a pair.

And to this day
when there's a Q
no question
U is there!

BUS STOP

KISS ME QUICK

QUACK!

Silly air

A and I are a silly pair.
See them floating in the air.
Next they're hiding in your chair,
then you find them in your hair.

The Rain in the Train

"Conductor! Conductor! I'd like to complain.
It's plain, there is rain, pouring into this train.
My paper is soggy, there's rain in my coffee,
it happened last week, now it's happened again!"

"Passenger, passenger, may I explain?
Our customers mainly delight in the rain.
They get a free cleaning and they arrive gleaming.
Now please take your seat
and stop being a pain!"

The Ch in Your Sneeze?

There's a ch in chocolate,
there's a ch in cheese.
There's a double ch in
cheeky chimpanzees.

There's a ch in champion,
a ch in chilli too.
But can you find the ch in sneeze?
It's there in your . . .

HAAAACHOOO!

The A in my Head!

"Doctor, should I go to bed?
I have an A inside my head.
Inside my head, I have an A.
It simply will not go away."

"Patient, what is that you say?
Inside your head you have an A?
Do not worry, you're OK:
every head is made that way!"

The Goat and the Toad

A gentleman goat
fell in love with a toad,
whom he happened to meet
by the side of the road.

He adored her low throat,
she adored his fur coat.
And so they were married,
the toad and the goat.

The Man in the Moon

The man in the moon
dropped into our school,
just yesterday morning
round about noon.

You may not believe me
but I have the proof:
there's a man-in-the-moon
shaped hole in the roof!

Ridiculous Ph

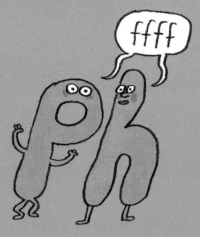

Ph goes ffff?
Can that really be?
Look at a telephone,
it's plain to see.
Look at an elephant,
look at a trophy,
look at a photograph
of Phil and Sophie.
Ph goes ffff,
it's ridiculous.
Add that fact to
your ridiculist!

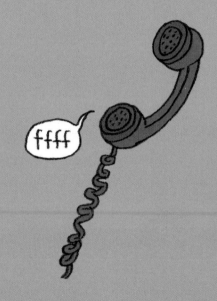

The Perfect Brown

Mrs Owl was after an evening gown.
A gown to match her feathery crown.
She looked in every store in town
and finally found the perfect brown.

Bow Wow

Said the cow to the dog, "please teach me how,
how I can learn to say bow wow."
"I'll teach you now," said the dog, "if you,
allow me in turn, to learn to moo."

Martha

Martha has a flying car.
She zooms around
from star to star,
with magic charms
packed up in jars.
She'd visit Earth
but it's just too far!

I-O-U-S are Furious!

I-O-U-S

can be serious.

They can also be mysterious.

I-O-U-S

can be curious.

But beware:

they can be FURIOUS!

Enough
of Uff

Uff, uff.

Do your stuff.

You're there in every

huff and puff.

But where are you

when things get tough?

Perhaps you felt you'd

had enough!

Cough

O-U-G-H

turns to off!
Every single time
you cough.

Suntan Lotion Commotion

T-I-O-N

caused a commotion
when they ran out
of suntan lotion.
"Stop!" said the policeman.
"Report to the station!"
"Sorry," they said,
"but we're on vacation."

"That," said the policeman,
"is no explanation.
Finishing a word is
your occupation.
Suntan lo_ _ _ _
is missing information.
Return to your bottle and
correct the situation."

T-I-O-N

had no hesitation.

"Sorry," they insisted.

"We have a reservation.

We're off to Paris

to concoct a potion.

Soon we'll be back to make

suntan lotion!"

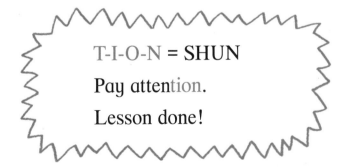

T-I-O-N = SHUN

Pay attention.

Lesson done!

Doing the Ing Thing

Whenever I-N-G
get together
they do the ing thing.
They like playing,
staying together,
doing the ing thing.
Singing, swinging,
and clapping in time,
eating, reading,
and rapping this rhyme,
they're in everything you do,
in something and in
nothing too.
Whenever I-N-G
get together,
they do the ing thing.

Secret Ears

You may wear sneakers
and a stripy cap.
You may wear jeans
that are faded and patched.
You may wear a dress
with a zip at the back.
But whatever you wear
has an ear attached!

Certainly a C

C is for cupcake,
C is for curtain.
C makes a C sound,
that is for certain.
But wait! Look at certain;
that's certainly a C
who seems to think
that she's an S,
as anyone can see!

S-P-L

When S-P-L
get together to chat,
S-P-L
make a splendid
SPLAT!

Why Should Should?

Why should should be

hard to spell?

Could could be

easier as well?

Why the O-U and the L?

If someone knows

would they please tell?

WOULD

SHOULD

COULD

_ _anks Very Much

Let's say, T-H went off one day.

How would we _ _ink of what to say?

We'd count our numbers differently.

Without them, we'd say: one, two, _ _ree.

You'd have two _ _umbs and that's not all:

how could a person _ _row a ball?

We'd all be very impolite.

_ _anks very much, just isn't right!

Bossy E

When E and A
get together,
E takes over
(E's ever so clever).
But A doesn't mind.
She takes a back seat
and gets on with eating
treat after treat.

A Very Short Lesson

Here's the lesson for today:

A + Y = ay.

That is all I have to say.

Lesson over. Go away!

Silent Letters
and
Secrets

You don't hear us when you whistle,
you don't hear us when you walk.
Hard as you may listen,
you won't hear us when you talk.
You don't hear us when you climb.
You won't hear us when you rhyme.
We are silent as you know,
but you see us all the time!

The B on
Your Thumb

Look, there's a B
right there on your thumb,
but of course you shouldn't mind . . .

For the B that you see
right there on your thumb
is not the stinging kind!

Doubt

I doubt you've ever thought about
the silent B in doubt.
I doubt that he's a happy B,
I bet he feels left out.
I doubt that life can be much fun
as a silent letter.
I do not doubt that B could be
doing something better!

The K on Your Knee

If you look down,

I think you'll see

a silent K

upon your knee.

Just sitting there

with nothing to say:

a silent K

that won't go away.

44

Now You Know

N-O spells no!
Easy peasy. Even so . . .
If you know something
that's know with a K.
And now you know
so that's OK!

Answer This!

What word has a silent W
right in the middle,
just to muddle you?
That is the question,
here is a clue:
the answer is actually
staring at you!

Who's There?

Knock, knock.
Who's there?
Who.
Who, who?
Who with a W,
sorry to trouble you!

Knock, knock.
Who's there?
Whoever.
Whoever who?
Whoever with a W,
but I'm not sure . . .
if this is actually
the right door!

Why Is That?

Where, what,

why, when.

Each W has

a silent friend.

Each has an H.

Each H is shy.

And no one knows

the reason why.

47

Day
and Ni_ _t

You can see

I-G-H-T

every single night.

But when you see

I-G-H-T

something isn't right.

Why should it be

that poor old G

never makes a sound?

Nor does the H, for heaven's sake,

they both just stand around!

If I were G and H

I would just disappear from sight

and leave the S and T to si_ _t

and worry day and ni_ _t.

A Secret Number

There's a word
you often say
with a secret number
tucked away.

The word is somewhere
in this rhyme:
it's find the
secret number time!

7 Secret Animals

There's a secret hen in when,
a secret cat in catch.
There's an owl inside your bowl
and a bat in every batch!

A delicious fish in selfish.
Every carpet has a pet.
There's a lion in a million.
Have you found them yet?

Christmas at the Castle

Meet the T of the castle
and H the castle ghost.
On Christmas day at half past two
they dine on crumbs of toast.

Spellings

Magic spells are powerful,
they're easy and they're quick.
You can cast a magic spell
once you learn the trick.

The E on Your Shoe

There is an E
on the tip of your shoe.
Just sitting there
with nothing to do.

Now take off your shoe
and what do you know?
Another E
on the end of your toe!

A Clue

Here's a clue
for words like blue:
ignore the E
and just say U.

Magical E

Magical E
has magical might.
See how she turns
a kit to a kite.
See how she turns
a tap into tape.
Abracadabra:
a cap is a ... cape!
She hops on a tub.
Now the tub is a tube.
Abracadabra ...
A dud is a ... dude!

A KIT FOR A KITE

Necessary

Princess Mary, Princess Mary,
tell me what is necessary?
C for curtsy, E double S.
"That's necessary," said the princess.

Definite

Just one F
then in and it.
Finish with E and
that's DEFINITE!

Separate

Separate
has two As.
They don't get on, it's true.
Luckily, there is an R
to sepaRate the two.

Different

D-I double F
(that's the start of it).
D-I double F . . .
(Er . . . what's the next bit?)
D-I double F . . .
(ER! Yes! I see!)
And then finally . . .
finish with E-N-T!

The Awful Rule

It's an awful rule
but it's beautiful as well:
any word that ends in ful
only has one L.

Take the ful in plateful
or the ful in frightful.
Any word that ends in ful
isn't ever quite full.

Weird

I before E
except after C
and W too,
on the odd occasion . . .
(Which is *weird*.)

The Most
Important

Anthony was an important Ant.
He knew he was oh-so important.
"No one can be as important as me,"
said Anthony Ant, most important.

Then Anthony Ant met Queen Antoinette,
an ant more important than he.
"I don't understand," wept Anthony Ant,
"how that could possibly be?"

A Lot

A lot is not
just one word.
It's always made of two.
A lot of people
don't know that.
From now on,
you do!

Banana

B-A-N-A-N-A.

It's nice to spell and say.
A monkey likes to eat a bunch
every single day.

Disappear

Make a pear disappear
using just your thumb,
in just 3 seconds:
3......... 2......... 1........!

The E-I in Their Jam

Spy the E-I in their jam! In their jam?

Spy the E-I in their ham. In their ham?

You can spy E-I in anything that's theirs.

Spy the E-I in their dotty underwear!

Rhyme
in a Rowboat

Mrs. R,
Mrs. H,
Mrs. Y and ME
took a rickety boat
across the sea.
Mrs. R she rowed,
Mrs. H helped out.
Mrs. Y and ME,
we yodeled about.

Here and There

Although you're standing over there
you're really very near.
For when you're standing over there
you're also standing here!

Words that Sound the Same
(Homophones)

"Hey green bean, how have you been?"
asked the friendly tangerine.
(Different words can sound alike.
It's hard to know what's write or right.)
She went and ate, eight ice-cream cones.
It's time to meet some homophones!

IT'S PLAIN
I AM A PLANE!

Two, Too, and To

Two, too, and to.
Three little 2s.
But how do you know
which to to use?
The number two
won't trouble you.
It always has
a W.

But if you mean
to say too much,
say something is
too hot to touch,
then too means
extra hot and so
you go and add
an extra O!

As for the third,
there's nothing to it.
Just one simple
O will do it.

Which Witch?

Which witch
is the which to use?
How do you know
which witch to use?
A wicked witch
has a wicked T,
as if to say
"Tee hee hee hee!"

Hear / Here

Dear, oh dear!

Is it here or hear?

The clue's in the word,

there is nothing to fear!

You HEAR with your ear.

That much is clear.

For "Come here to me,"

it's just E-R-E.

A
Whole
Donut

Take a whole donut
and what do you find?
A whole donut
has a hole inside!
A whole donut
means the entire thing.
The hole in the middle
is the empty ring.

Dreadful Weather

The weather is dreadful.

Each day is the same.

It's always

Wind-E And THunder-E Rain.

Whether

Whether you're short,
whether you're tall,
whether you're big,
whether you're small,
find out whether you can see
whether this kind of whether
has a hidden he.

Getting the most out of the rhyme

After reading a rhyme, spend a few minutes with your child, exploring the learning concept behind it.

To do this, you can do a simple activity together. Here are some easy ideas on which you can build.

1. MAKE A LIST TOGETHER, THEN CHOP IT UP!

Use any old paper, scissors, and 2 bright marker pens.

Work as a team. Spend a few minutes creating a list of 6–10 words which share the same sounds or letter group as the ones explored in the rhyme. You should both contribute to the list. Give your child hints to help them think of suitable words.

For example, for AY write down AY words: day, say, play, lay, may, stay, today, okay, hooray

Write the words in nice big letters then cut the list into separate word slips. Your child can have fun helping with this.

TRY THIS WITH THESE RHYMES:

- BOSSY E
- I-O-U-S ARE FURIOUS
- THE AWFUL RULE
- THE STORY OF Q AND U
- A VERY SIMPLE LESSON
- RIDICULOUS PH
- O-U ARE INSIDE OUT
- DOING THE ING THING
- SUNTAN LOTION COMMOTION
- DAY AND NI___T

Spread the word slips on the floor around you then take turns saying a sentence that includes one of the word slips. Pick up the word slip you're using and wave it overhead. Pick up speed! Continue until all the word slips have been collected.

If you use the word slip at the end of the sentence, you'll create a rhyme together. For instance:

> You: Would you like to come and stay?
> Child: I'll ask my mother if I may.
> You: I hope that it will be okay.
> Child: In the meantime, let's just play.

2. RUNAWAY LETTERS

Focus on the cluster sound covered in the rhyme. Work as a team to make a list of words which include that sound cluster. Help your child contribute to the list. For example, for 'Th' you might include, thick, thought and thumb.

What if those letters ran off one day? Try chatting together without saying those sounds, e.g.: "ick," "ought," and "umb!"

TRY THIS WITH THESE RHYMES:

- __ANKS VERY MUCH
- THE SH IN YOUR SHOE
- THE CH IN YOUR SNEEZE?

3. BE A MAGICIAN,
TURN HERE INTO THERE

Write down **here** on a slip of paper.
Write a **t** on another slip.
Join them up and . . .
Hey presto: here is there!

Now let your child be the teacher
and show you how it's done!

TURN A TUB INTO A TUBE

Write down word slips for:
tub, mat, kit, mit, bit, can, dud*.
Write an E on another slip.
Join them up and . . .
Hey presto: a dud is a dude!

*Have some fun explaining
the meanings of both
"dud" and "dude!"

4. WHAT IF SILENT LETTERS COULD SPEAK?

Explain some letters make no sound.
(They just seem to hang around.)
What if these letters weren't so meek?
What if they had a chance to speak?

Write down the silent letter word/s
from the rhyme. Use a different color
for the silent letters. Now take turns
saying the word in a new way: by
sounding the silent letter!

TRY THIS WITH THESE RHYMES:

- DOUBT
- CHRISTMAS AT THE CASTLE
- THE B ON YOUR THUMB
- WHO'S THERE?
- THE K ON YOUR KNEE
- ANSWER THIS
- WHY IS THAT?

Add extra toppings

Once your child is familiar with a rhyme you can add handclaps, physical motions, or a simple tune.

5. HAND CLAPPING A RHYME

The words included in the spellings section of this book are actually the same words that commonly trip up adults. (This fact may amuse your child!) By learning these spellings as rhythmic handclapping chants, you'll help your child remember them.

Turn any of these rhymes into a simple hand clapping chant for two people, patty-cake style. (Clap your hands on the one and your child's on the two.)

One and two and three and four.
That's the rhythm (nothing more).
Clap your hands, and now clap hers.
Keep this up as you say the words.

TRY THIS WITH THESE RHYMES:

- NECESSARY
- DIFFERENT
- DEFINITE
- BANANA
- RHYME IN A ROWBOAT
- WEATHER

THIS CAN ALSO WORK FOR:

- A SHORT LESSON
- O-U ARE INSIDE OUT

6. GET PHYSICAL!

As you read a rhyme, have your child do physical actions
to mark the sound or letter patterns as you say them. For instance:

Jump for ants with Anthony Ant
Every time that there's a word with an ant,
do a little jump and wave your hands.

The Rain in the Train
Hands on heads for each AI word.

Who's there?
Mark each silent W by making a W,
(using both thumbs and pointer fingers).

Doing the Ing Thing
Stand up and sit down again for every ING sound.

*Note: For the word "necessary,"
have fun demonstrating a curtsy!*

**TRY THIS WITH
THESE RHYMES:**

- THE MOST IMPORTANT
- RAIN IN THE TRAIN
- WHO'S THERE?
  DOING THE ING THING
- MAN ON THE MOON

Spy the E-I

Turn this into a simple song which your child will already know using the tune of "Head, Shoulders, Knees, and Toes."

"Spy" replaces "Head."
"The E–I' replaces "Shoulders."
"In their jam" replaces "Knees and toes."

The Ch in Your Sneeze
& The Sh in Your Shoe

These can both be sung to the tune of: *Miss Lucy had a Baby, she named him Tiny Tim . . .*

TRY THIS WITH THESE RHYMES:

- SPY THE E-I
- THE CH IN YOUR SNEEZE
- THE SH IN YOUR SHOE